30-day Journey to Self-Love

By Tamiko Lynn

This Journal is inspired by & dedicated to my mother Myla Veland and my grandmothers Glady Marie Veland-Morris & Katie Mae Thompson. My sister Ericka Veland, my granddaughter Samiya Le'von Hardnett & my bonus granddaughter Lyric Marie Charles

Daughters: Tiara Hardnett, Tiana Hardnett, & my bonus daughter Jamye Mitchell
Sons- Joseph Jones Jr. & bonus son Jaxson Hussman

My aunts: Melissa Dean, Rhonda Oliver, Leta Veland, Lisa Veland, Eva Veland & Cherie Veland

History Teacher: Trish Sheppard
First Lady: Angela Banks
Mentor: Monique Jenkins
Life Coach: Wyvonne Harper

© 2025 Tlynn Productions LLC
No part of this publication may be reproduced, distributed, or transmitted in any form or by any means, including photocopying, recording, or other electronic or mechanical methods, or by any information storage and retrieval system without the prior written permission of the publisher, except in the case of very brief quotations embodied in critical reviews and certain other noncommercial uses permitted by copyright law

ISBN: 979-8-218-59094-9
LCCN: 2025900424

Anytime you feel frustrated just pick up this Journal!
Mya Brewer, Aliyah William, Kalliyan Veland, Brooklyn Veland, Amaziah Cauthen, Carlee Rose, KaNiya Belgrave, Arey'Onna Saunsoci, Journee Holley, My'Auna Henderson, Malasia Jackson, P. Koehler, Zee, K. Flores, Chantell Gerard, Callie Sokoll, Aries F.N., Isabella Grassia, & Madisyn Stark.

INTRODUCTION

I remember when I was about 7 years old, there was a neighborhood girl who I thought was so beautiful that every time I saw her, my eyes would light up. One day, I saw her walking with her friend, and I looked up to see them sitting beside me on the neighborhood park bench. I was so happy that someone I admired was sitting so close to me.

They both began to giggle after looking at me, and the girl I thought was beautiful asked her friend, "Who is this ugly little girl smiling at me?"

At that moment, I thought to myself, *"I'm ugly."*

I sat there and cried until all my tears were dry because I didn't want my parents to ask me why I was crying.

I never spoke about the daily teasing and jokes that were made about me in elementary and junior high school. I couldn't wrap my mind around why my parents thought I was so pretty. I would often tell myself, *"They're only saying that because they don't want to hurt my feelings."*

As I got older, I realized that this was the beginning of me protecting other people's emotions and putting how I felt on the back burner.

You couldn't pay me to think that I was something special.

Although my parents lived in separate households, I knew they both loved me. As I grew, I realized that they each had their own individual way of showing me their version of love.

At an early age, I felt that I was gifted and had a purpose here on Earth, but I didn't know what it was. All I was focused on at the time was how much I hated being teased in school for my buck-toothed smile and my stuttering speech impediment.

According to the world, I was considered ugly, and I believed it.

I would often cry myself to sleep, and in those moments, my spirit felt like I didn't belong on this Earth. I convinced myself that I was a mistake.

One thing I regret is that I was too afraid to express my feelings. Even if I had told at least one person, especially my parents, maybe I would have grown beyond my fears. But I was too ashamed.

I believe that every single person in this world has experienced some type of defeat or sadness related to growing pains. When we're young, we often think that adults don't go through growing pains, but they do, and in ways we could never imagine. We believe they're supposed to have all the answers, but in reality, they're learning those answers through the challenges life presents. Mistakes aren't failures, they are opportunities to become a better person.

This journal is designed to help you look past your own insecurities and begin to understand just how amazing you truly are.
Although I've finally learned how amazing I was and still am, it took me years...
I don't want you to wait that long!

Welcome to your 30-day Journey to Self-Love.

Today, you've decided to challenge yourself by taking a deeper look at who you are. Understanding who you truly are and learning how to set boundaries in your life is one of the most important decisions you will ever make. Believe it or not, most adults don't tackle this topic until many years down the line. The fact that you're starting this journey early is the right thing to do, but I don't want to limit this journey to a specific age. If you're older, I welcome you to this journey as well.

What I want you to understand is that the choices you make throughout your life will determine the direction in which you head as you grow.

Are you ready to discover the true beauty of being self-aware and headed in the right direction? The first step in your journey involves holding yourself accountable for three key factors.

#1. The mistakes you've made

#2. What you feel others may have done to you.

#3. Letting go of what you cannot control.

This journal is designed for every type of living situation. Whether you have wealthy parents, foster parents, or parents who struggle financially, whether you're in a single-parent home, a juvenile detention center, on probation, or living in an orphanage—this journal is for you.

Every morning, we will meditate.

Meditation means: To think deeply or focus one's mind for a period, either in silence or with the aid of chanting, for religious, spiritual purposes, or as a method of relaxation. Every day, I want you to wake up and speak the following words aloud **twice**:

- **I am beautiful**
- **I am loved**
- **I can do anything I put my mind too**
- **I am special**
- **I can overcome any obstacle**
- **I am destined**
- **I will not believe negative words**
- **I am worthy**

When I started my own personal journey, a wise man once told me this: "Every day, I want you to grab a pen and write down anything you can remember about yourself. Whether it's about your childhood or where you are now." He said that one of the hardest tasks a person will face is learning how to focus on themselves. So, by taking at least 10 minutes out of your day to write about *you* and only *you*, this will force you to think about *yourself* and no one else.

Great advice. Thank you, Brother Larry Duncan.

Make a promise to yourself to use this journal every day

When you write down your feelings, be sure to answer everything truthfully.
What good does it do to lie to yourself?

Now is the time to start living in your truth.

There is a *Storytime* section in the journal, featuring true stories meant to inspire. Hearing someone else's story has the potential to heal and motivate.

Keep in mind that their story may not resonate with you, but I'm sure someone else can relate.

It's always powerful to hear about people who have overcome tough times, because you never know if you'll face a similar obstacle down the line.

Do your weekly activities, and don't be afraid to include an adult in the process.

You may just learn something about them you didn't know.

JOURNALING

Before you begin this process, I'd like you to spend the first day writing down your thoughts.

You can write about something fun, something that makes you happy or sad, just spend the day learning how to journal.

Journaling helps decrease anger and anxiety, and it promotes self-reflection. When I look back at some of my Facebook memories, I can see how far I've come.

I don't post personal information often, but when I do, it's kept to a minimum.

Always remember that most people are looking for entertainment.

Choose not to be a clown in someone else's circus. This is why learning how to journal is so important. It teaches you how to talk to yourself instead of relying on social media. Social media can often come back to bite you in the end.

There's nothing wrong with talking to yourself and listening to that inner voice that helps you distinguish right from wrong.

MY THOUGHTS

LIST THE MONTH, DAY, TIME, AND YEAR BELOW!

Your first activity is to write down **5** things you love about yourself and **5** things you dislike

SIDE NOTE: It doesn't have to be your outer appearance.

Example: You may not like your own attitude. Being honest about your own hangups will remind you of what you need to change.

1
2
3
4
5

1
2
3
4
5

I am unapologetically a woman

"Doesn't mean that I am perfect.

It means that I will not compromise the steps that it took to become this woman.
I've made several wrong turns before I started making the right ones.
And this integrity that I have now was built on the mistakes of the past.

So, since you did not give it to me, you are less qualified to take it away. We don't apologize; we simply adjust.
Rather than adjusting your own crown, or ignoring the crowd, balancing our energy, and avoiding the clowns, we as women hold the weight of the world on our shoulders. Sometimes in heels, or maybe in gym shoes.
But hear me clearly:
ONLY TO OUR DESTINY ARE WE TO YIELD"

Wyvonne Harper

Day 1

REPEAT TWICE EVERY MORNING

- I am beautiful
- I am loved
- I can do anything I put my mind too
- I am special
- I can overcome any obstacle
- I am destined
- I will not believe negative words
- I am worthy

You woke up this morning.
But guess what?

Someone didn't wake up this morning, and yet, you were given the gift of life today. To be able to look at life through a different lens and learn helpful tools for your personal growth are just a few of the reasons I created this journal.

You may be going through a tough time right now, but remember, growing up comes with its obstacles. There's no easy way to escape life's tough moments.
Check this out: According to the CDC (Centers for Disease Control), approximately 12,000 children and young adults ages 1-19 die each year from unintentional injuries, motor vehicle accidents, suicide, and homicide. Unintentional injuries are one of the leading causes of non-fatal injuries for children aged 10-14.
Homicide is the second leading cause of death for teens aged 15-19.

I could go on and on, but do you see why I asked if you were excited to wake up this morning? I wanted to give you a clear picture of where you are today.
There are days when we wake up filled with joy, the sun is shining, everything seems to be falling into place. You might be looking forward to eating at your favorite restaurant or hanging out with your best friend. It feels like it's going to be a wonderful day.

Then there are those days when we wake up feeling like the world is on our shoulders. We don't feel like getting out of bed. Despite having slept well, we're angry, sad, or confused. When confusion creeps in, we must remind ourselves that someone else is so sick or so troubled that they couldn't get out of bed today.

And for that reason alone, that should be enough to make us hop out of bed, right? Well, sometimes, that's not how life works. We all have these moments, young or old, it doesn't matter.

Start your day with a plan in mind and commit to following through. Turn off social media and take a moment to regroup your thoughts. We have the power to create the kind of day we want to have.

For example, there might be a teacher or a supervisor who works your last nerve. I'm sure they understand this too, so they might call your name to answer a question or assign you a task, and you immediately feel that irritation rising. You might catch yourself mumbling,

"Please don't let this person get on my nerves today."

Well, if you've ever muttered those words to yourself, guess what? You gave yourself a heads-up by acknowledging what might trigger you and choosing to remain calm. You knew that this person had the potential to upset you, so you used self-talk to remind yourself of what you were up against.

Here is your First exercise

Write down how you are feeling this morning. Whether it's good or bad, write down your thoughts. I want you to look back at this one day and see your growth. This will be your personal keepsake and diary.

Day 2

- I am beautiful
- I am loved
- I can do anything I put my mind too
- I am special
- I can overcome any obstacle
- I am destined
- I will not believe negative words
- I am worthy

Today's Lesson: **Self Care**

Self-care is extremely important because the way you treat yourself reflects how others will treat you. When you take care of yourself, you also teach others how to treat you. It's hard to see the beauty in others when you don't see it within yourself.

After a shower, always apply lotion to moisturize your skin. Your skin is a barrier, serving as one of the body's first lines of defense against harmful bacteria. Keeping your skin moisturized not only hydrates it but also seals in moisture. Plus, applying lotion after every bath gives your skin a healthy glow and a soft feel. There's nothing better than a woman's glowing skin. It'll make you feel good inside, and your skin will thank you for it.

As you get older, you'll come to appreciate having beautiful, soft, well-cared-for skin. If you have oil or perfume, use them after your shower. Grab some emery boards to file your nails and make sure your fingers and toes are even and clean. Be sure to clean out the bathtub after you're done and keep your space organized. Straighten up your bed when you wake up.

Make it a point to look your best before heading to school or leaving the house. It doesn't take much money to look decent. Iron your clothes if they're wrinkled and apply your favorite lip gloss. You may not have the luxury of visiting a hairstylist every week but make the most of what you have.

Self-care depends on the natural state in which you exist. In other words, if you don't have all the finer things in life, that's okay. Your beauty is about what's inside and how you perceive yourself. If you do have those luxuries, this still applies to you. Luxuries come with hard work and patience. Focus on being grateful for whatever situation you're in right now. At the end of the day, someone cares about you enough to have shared this journal with you. Here are some additional examples of self-care beyond your regular daily routine:

- Listening to your favorite song with your headphones on
- Read a book
- Cooking a healthy meal or a smoothie
- Take a walk or exercise for 30 minutes a day (if you don't play sports or go to the gym)
- Making sure you get a good night's rest
- Hang up the phone at night
- Staying far away from gossip
- Writing your morning thoughts down in a Diary
- Pray/Meditate
- Dancing/Singing
- Reading and taking part in this Journal

Write down 5 self-care daily goals that you will commit to for the next 30 days and stick to them.

1)

2)

3)

4)

5)

Day 3

- I am beautiful
- I am loved
- I can do anything I put my mind too
- I am special
- I can overcome any obstacle
- I am destined
- I will not believe negative words
- I am worthy

Today's lesson: Beauty is only skin deep

Have you ever met someone who was pleasing to the eyes, but when they spoke, you could immediately tell they were mean-spirited or angry? That's a perfect example of the saying, *"beauty is only skin deep."* Real beauty comes from within.

As you grow into your womanhood, you'll begin to pay less attention to what someone looks like on the outside and start to appreciate what's inside.

We often admire people who appear to have it all together, but are they truly beautiful on the inside? Do they smile genuinely and speak kindly, or do they walk around with a chip on their shoulder, pretending to be happy? Are they rude? Angry? Why do they seem mad all the time?

Often, those who project anger are suffering in silence. They might look stunning to the eyes, but inside, they are hurting. Their pain is projected onto others. How can they treat someone else kindly when they don't even like who they are?

One of the most powerful lessons my grandmother taught me was this: *"Treat people how you would like to be treated."*

But here's the flip side: Just because someone has had a tough time doesn't give them the right to take out their frustrations on others. They might see people who seem to have it all together, but we don't know what struggles those people face. What glitters isn't always gold.

Another quote from my grandmother that sticks with me: *"The same people you see going up are the same ones you'll see coming down."*

What she meant was that life has its ups and downs. One day, you might run into someone who seemed to have nothing, but later in life, they've blossomed. Sometimes, the people who seemed to have nothing really had it all. They may not have had financial resources, but they were given tools to create a better future for themselves. They worked hard, executed a plan, and stuck to it.

Another quote she shared was: *"You never know who might have to give you a glass of water."*

Can you treat someone kindly who doesn't have anything to offer you right now?

I've been a nurse for 21 years, and I remember reading a list of new patients that arrived over the weekend. To my surprise, one of them was someone I went to school with. Although I was eager to greet her with a smile and do everything I could to help, I never imagined I would one day be her nurse. We both came from the same neighborhood, but somewhere along the way, she was introduced to drugs.

When I walked into her room, I saw the shame in her eyes, but I treated her with kindness, love, and grace. She didn't deserve to feel judged.

There was another time I had a run-in with a judge. I had been caught shoplifting when I was younger, and he was the judge who sentenced me. Years later, I arrived at work, looked at my list of patients, and guess who it was? The same judge.

He didn't remember me, but as soon as I walked into his room, he started giving me tasks. "Honey, can you get me some water and a blanket?" he said, treating me like I was his personal assistant.

I said, "You don't remember me, but you were the judge who sentenced me when I was 18." He was stunned. "Oh my goodness, honey, I hope I was nice to you?" he asked.

I smiled and said, "Yes, you were nice, as nice as you were allowed to be. But now, I hold the gavel!" He laughed, cried, and gave me the tightest hug I've ever received from a patient.

When he left, he thanked me over and over again. He told me how happy he was that he hadn't mistreated me, and as he got older, he often worried about how he treated people in his courtroom.

You never know who you'll face down the line. People change, situations change, and life is full of unexpected turns.

Remember: outer appearances don't show the true essence of a person's heart. What truly matters are their actions. You never know someone's full story. I grew up around people who, based on their appearance, would've never guessed the trauma they'd experienced as children.

Make a commitment to focus on building your character. It's not easy to look inside and promote change, but when you make a mistake or act out of character, acknowledge it, apologize, and keep trying. Eventually, you'll see the growth.

A few examples of good character traits are:

- Compassionate
- Reliable
- Respectful
- Forgiving
- Honesty

WHO ARE YOU?
WHAT ARE A FEW OF YOUR POSITIVE CHARACTER TRAITS?

1)
2)
3)
4)
5)

WHICH CHARACTER TRAITS DO YOU NEED TO WORK ON?

1)
2)
3)
4)
5)

Challenge Time

Stand in front of the mirror, completely naked. Take a moment to look at the body you were born with. Grab those love handles and embrace your beauty. Stare at yourself from top to bottom for a full five minutes. If you don't have love handles, rub your flat tummy and embrace your body.
This is who you are at this moment.

Do you hate your body?
If your answer is yes, remember, this is something that can be changed.

It will require discipline, but with exercise and changes to your diet, you can transform. However, as with everything else, it all starts in the mind. You must be willing to change, to grow, and to become better. The way your body looks right now is not as important as how you feel on the inside. When you begin to love yourself, you'll start to embrace the qualities you once thought you disliked about yourself. Embracing your flaws will give you the power and motivation to change. Sometimes, those flaws are only seen by you. I've pointed out my flaws to others, and they didn't even notice them.

I can guarantee that 30 years from now, you'll look back at your younger self and say, "Wow, I looked amazing." You may want bigger legs, a fuller butt, straighter teeth, longer hair, smaller breasts, or a larger chest—the list could go on. But ask yourself: What good is a great body if my mind isn't healthy?
Remember, you are uniquely designed, and there is no one on this earth better than you.

Write down how you felt after you finished reading the last chapter.

What would you like to change?

What is your favorite feature on your body?

> "Do the best you can until you know better.
> Then when you know better, do better."
>
> Maya Angelou

"**Our deepest fear** is not that we are inadequate. Our deepest fear is that we are powerful beyond measure. It is our light, not our darkness that most frightens us. We ask ourselves, who am I to be brilliant, gorgeous, talented, fabulous? Actually, who are you not to be? You are a child of God. Your playing small does not serve the world. There is nothing enlightening about shrinking so that other people won't feel insecure around you. We are all meant to shine, as children do. We were born to make manifest the glory of God that is within us. It's not just in some of us; it's in everyone. And as we let our own light shine, we unconsciously give other people permission to do the same. As we are liberated from our own fear, our presence automatically liberates others."

Marianne Williamson

Day 4

- I am beautiful
- I am loved
- I can do anything I put my mind too
- I am special
- I can overcome any obstacle
- I am destined
- I will not believe negative words
- I am worthy

Today's lesson: Fear

Let's take a deeper look at the quote from the movie *Coach Carter* on the previous page.
I was an adult when I first heard this, and it really stuck with me. To sum it up, the quote highlights how we sometimes shrink ourselves to make others feel comfortable.
For example, you might have a friend who's great at sports or dancing—skills that you also possess or would love to learn. Instead of showcasing your own talent, though, you decide to keep it to yourself.
Why?
Is it fear?
Maybe you're afraid they'll judge you or say something negative about your abilities. You might worry that others will gossip, whispering things like, "Oh, she just wants to be like me."
So, what happens next?

You end up shrinking yourself. The more you hide your gifts, the angrier you become. Sometimes, we redirect that anger toward others because of our own fear. Unknowingly, we start blaming the people who love us, simply because we didn't have the courage to push through our fears.

When I was growing up, I knew I could sing, but my cousin wasn't afraid to sing. So, for years, I would just sit and watch her, too scared of rejection to sing myself. I would see how my grandmother's eyes would light up when my cousin sang her favorite gospel songs, but there I was, paralyzed by fear.

I didn't sing in front of anyone because of my fear. It took me years to understand what was holding me back.

So, my question for you today is: What talents are you hiding from others or even from your own parents because of fear?

Take a moment to write down the talents you have, or the ones you'd like to learn.

Day 5

- I am beautiful
- I am loved
- I can do anything I put my mind too
- I am special
- I can overcome any obstacle
- I am destined
- I will not believe negative words
- I am worthy

Today's lesson: What are your gifts?

I spent most of my childhood hiding the fact that I could sing, afraid to let anyone hear me. Even though I thought I sounded great, I didn't believe anyone else would like it. I was afraid to be great.

Ask yourself: **Are you afraid to be great?
Are you afraid of rejection?**

It's okay to be afraid, but it's not okay to live in fear. Fear is a natural human reaction, but when you allow it to become a part of who you are, you're living in a constant state of fear. Until you take that leap, you will always find yourself circling back to fear instead of moving toward the greatness within you.

For example, I was fearful writing this journal entry. I doubted myself every time I thought about it. My mind was full of questions: *What if it doesn't help anyone? What if I don't explain things well enough? What if I share too much?* These self-doubting thoughts would race through my mind every single time I sat down to type. But I had to take a leap and push past the fear.

As I type this today, I am moving forward despite the fear. The desire to accomplish something in life must be greater than your fear of failure.

You know you can do it, but it's hard to take that leap of faith. So, let's start the healing process now and break the cycle.

After you've thought **deeply** about your gifts and talents, write them down.

CHALLENGE TIME

Tell someone about your gifts and talents.

How do you expect anyone to help nurture your gifts if they don't even know you have them?

Once they're aware of your desires and dreams, you'll start to mentally move toward making them become a reality. Every dream begins as a thought before it turns into action.

The first step is always acknowledgment.

Talk to someone you feel comfortable with. They can help you nurture and shape your thoughts, offering support as you work toward your dreams.

Later in this journal, I've included a fun activity to help you become more familiar with your own gifts and talents

Day 6

- I am beautiful
- I am loved
- I can do anything I put my mind too
- I am special
- I can overcome any obstacle
- I am destined
- I will not believe negative words
- I am worthy

Story Time

At an early age I would watch one of my favorite aunts work as a nurse. There was something about wearing that white jacket, looking pretty, and taking care of people that made me happy. My mother was on drugs heavy, so when I was at home, I would beg to go over my grandmother's house. I heard the same answer every time, no.
I had to make sure I took care of my siblings so it was very seldom that she would allow me to go. My father was also on drugs, but he was more functional. My dad and mom were a one-night stand, but he would try his best to give me what little money he could. He was married to a woman who hated me because I looked just like my mother and that brought back memories of how he cheated on her with my mother.
Often when he would call me, I heard her being verbally aggressive in the background. Later I found out that he had a mental breakdown and checked himself in a drug facility in another state.

As I got older, I realized that lady did not like herself, she was scorned. I was so proud of my dad for getting away from her.

After a while I joined a neighborhood gang. These girls were fun to be around and since my mother stayed in the streets, my home became a place where everyone would meet. I was young but I learned how to cook, and the local drug dealers would purchase food for me to cook for my siblings and our friends. Sometimes they would help with the bills, and it felt like a family but being around them influenced me to make some bad decisions. I was

18 years old and no matter what my circumstances were, I kept good grades. My goal was to become a nurse, and I wanted to make it out of the hood to help my siblings and hopefully make my mother proud enough to shake the drugs. I was not into boys at this time because I was molested by one of the neighborhood kids, but I never told anyone. That situation made me hate boys. I was the cool girl, and my male friends knew I was a tom boy. Although they would sometimes whisper about my womanly figure, they never tried to have sex with me. Well just two months shy of graduation, I was busted selling crack to an undercover police officer. I felt like my life was over. How will I take care of my siblings, where will I be able to work with this on my criminal history? What am I going to do? I was so confused.

My siblings were placed into foster care and my mother blamed me. The mother of one of my close friends allowed me to stay with them but I had to get a job to help with the bills. I was hired at a local grocery store that hired felons, but I started selling drugs again because I had already become addicted to fast cash and the grocery store wasn't paying much. Once again, I was busted and was sentenced to prison. I spent two years there and since I had good behavior I was transferred to a treatment facility.
One thing I was proud of is that I received my GED before I was released.

While I was at this treatment center, I met a lady that I will call Ms. C.
Ms. C. was 65 years old. She had been incarcerated her whole life for something that she did when she was twenty-five. She didn't know what she was about to do. She did not want to be free at this point because she had no skills, no family, and was afraid to live outside of prison. I got to know her and realized that she was wise and had a beautiful spirit. One thing she said to me that I will never forget was you are not what you have been through, and you have plenty of time to change. It is going to take patience but look in the mirror and tell yourself that you are worth it.
Every day she would say things that would motivate me. Every time I would go look for a job, I would be so excited to come back and tell her about the progress I had made. I used to catch the bus, which was new, but it felt so good. I felt free. I was able to talk to my siblings and my life felt amazing because I was determined to change.

I received a note from the warden and was told that my mother had passed away. As I was on my way back to my room, I learned that Ms. C. went to the hospital and passed away. My mother passed away after she smoked drugs one night and I honestly believe that Mrs. C. died from a broken heart. She didn't want to be free but, once again, I felt extreme sadness and was alone and afraid. I wanted to give up.
I had not spoken to my father, and I heard he had relapsed. The drugs ruined my family.

My family and friends had their own lives to deal with. They were either married with children, on drugs, dead or in jail. I really didn't want to become a burden and interfere with what anyone else had going on.

After a few weeks of constant tears and sadness, I woke up one morning and decided I cannot give up. Ms. C. made me believe that I could be somebody. I honestly didn't believe it, but I thought maybe I should give it a try. I mean what did I have to lose?

There was a pastor who would come to the halfway house and preach. I never went to listen but, on this day, I was so mentally weak that I went to that service and the rest was history.
He taught me the word of God, and his wife began to mentor me. She said she saw something in me. She showed me proper etiquette and how to speak with eloquence. Her friends were also doing well in life, and they offered to help with anything I needed. One lady offered to pay for me to take a course that would certify me to become a Provisional alcohol and drug counselor. It was an entry wage earning position, but I was able to visit my siblings regularly, take them on outings and they could visit me at my own apartment.
To complete my story, I decided to keep furthering my education. I became a licensed mental health therapist.

I got married and had four beautiful children and began living a life that I never thought I could. Seems like everyone I met after I got into trouble has helped shaped me into the woman I am today. It all made sense. Where would I be if I had not gone through those obstacles and met those people along the way? It felt like they were angels.

The moral of my story is, never ever stop believing in yourself. Life didn't come with a handbook and sometimes the hand you were dealt isn't fair, but keep working hard, respect your journey, and try to learn as much as you can and things will work out fine.

Day 7

- I am beautiful
- I am loved
- I can do anything I put my mind too
- I am special
- I can overcome any obstacle
- I am destined
- I will not believe negative words
- I am worthy

JOURNAL DAY

Spend the day journaling and focusing on you!

MY THOUGHTS

MY THOUGHTS

Day 8

- I am beautiful
- I am loved
- I can do anything I put my mind too
- I am special
- I can overcome any obstacle
- I am destined
- I will not believe negative words
- I am worthy

Today's lesson: The Art of Listening

Listening can be incredibly difficult when you're young, and it often becomes even harder as you grow older. I'm guilty of this too, but before anyone can achieve true success, they must learn how to listen.

Have you ever heard the saying, "A hard head makes a soft behind"? It may sound like it's referring to a spanking, but it's about how life will "whip your tail" when you don't listen to your elders. Ultimately, choosing not to listen can hurt you in the long run.

Our elders have made plenty of mistakes, and in some cases, they may not have all the answers, but they love us.

When you're fortunate enough to receive advice or wisdom from someone, the greatest gift you can give yourself is to really listen.

No matter how annoying the information may seem, challenge yourself to listen. Even if it sounds irrational or confusing, just listen.

It's always your choice to make the right decisions and take the right actions, but at least you'll have heard the options. You can't blame your elders when you had the privilege of hearing advice and chose not to take it.

If you know someone making poor decisions as an adult, keep in mind that this person either didn't listen when they were younger, or they weren't given the right tools and simply don't know any better.

Poor listening leads to miscommunication, assumptions, and ineffective decision-making.

Here's a few quotes regarding listening:

"No one is as deaf as the person who will not listen"
Author Unknown

"One of the sincerest forms of respect is actually listening to what another has to say" **Bryant H. McGill**

"Most of the successful people I've known are the ones who do more listening than talking" **Benard M. Baruch**

Then there are the people who don't listen to hear you out; they listen only to respond. They'll call you and ask what you're doing, and if you say "nothing," they'll immediately start unloading everything on their mind for the day.

A conversation requires two people. In that moment, you may not be doing anything, but you might still need someone to talk to. However, these types of people believe that what's going on in their minds is far more important than what's on yours. There's nothing worse than pouring your feelings out to someone and feeling unheard.

When someone doesn't respect you enough to listen to what you have to say, but will happily unpack all their thoughts on you, you have two options:

1. **Ask them to listen.**
2. **Stop the conversation.**

This helps prevent you from becoming angry, because at the end of the day, the only person you can control is yourself. When someone can't listen while others are speaking, it shows poor concentration, lack of interest, and selfishness.

We all deserve to be heard, to have a voice, and to feel that our opinions are valued.

CHALLENGE TIME

Seek out an adult—whether it's a teacher, parent, foster parent, a friend's parent, or any trusted adult. Ask them about a time when they failed to listen and what the consequence of that action was.

This challenge is designed to help you focus on listening to **understand**, not just listening to respond.

During this challenge, be sure to:
- **Stay quiet** and give them your full attention.
- **Make eye contact** and truly focus on what they're saying.
- **Be patient**, as adults can sometimes be long-winded (which means they may go on and on!).

As simple as this task may seem, you'll find that by taking the time to listen without judgment, both you and the adult will experience the joy of a genuine connection.

You never know the last time that person has had the chance to speak and feel heard.

After the conversation, take a moment to reflect.

- **Write down your thoughts** about the conversation.
- Did you learn anything from hearing their story?

Day 9

- I am beautiful
- I am loved
- I can do anything I put my mind too
- I am special
- I can overcome any obstacle
- I am destined
- I will not believe negative words
- I am worthy

Today's lesson: Boundaries

The Definition of Boundaries
(out of bounds)
A boundary is a line that marks the limit of an area dividing line.

How does that definition apply to us?

Without setting boundaries, we leave the door open for others to violate our space and treat us however they want. When you set boundaries for yourself, you're showing others what you will and won't tolerate.

Often, when someone challenges your boundaries, it's a reflection of their own poor sense of self-worth.

Here's an example:
Let's say you have a friend who is Muslim, and you've shared with them that you study Christianity. You've expressed that you avoid religious debates because you're firm in your faith. Then, the very next day, they bring up the topic again. Now they've crossed the line because you were clear about your beliefs.

I used religion as an example because, in today's world, it's a heavy and controversial topic. It's wise to avoid debates about beliefs. If your belief system changes, that's okay too. But if someone repeatedly disregards your boundaries, they need to be limited to less serious conversations. At that point, it's clear they don't respect you.

When your boundaries are consistently crossed, ask yourself: Is it worth continuing the relationship with this person, or should you let them go? Giving someone who constantly oversteps too many chances will only lead to frustration. You'll get upset with yourself for allowing them to continue being a part of your life. If they've done it once, chances are, they'll do it again.

Another example:
Some people love to touch you while they talk, but maybe you have a personal space boundary. You don't feel comfortable when someone touches you or gets too close. It's important to express that. If you give someone an inch, they'll take a mile—but remember, no one can read your mind. It's perfectly okay to say, "Hey, I'm not really a touchy-feely person."

You can set boundaries in every area of your life.

Expect to receive pushback now and then. If you set a boundary that causes someone to walk away, **let them walk**. Sometimes, it's a sign that the relationship wasn't healthy to begin with.

> "You can always tell how mature someone is based on the amount of grace they extend."
>
> Wyvonne Harper

Day 10

- I am beautiful
- I am loved
- I can do anything I put my mind too
- I am special
- I can overcome any obstacle
- I am destined
- I will not believe negative words
- I am worthy

Today's lesson: Grace

It took me a while to understand how to extend grace to myself. Anytime trauma enters our lives, we must learn to extend grace to ourselves, so we don't drown in pain, embarrassment, or shame. It's okay to be upset, but there's no need to be too hard on ourselves. Extending grace means acknowledging that it's okay to make mistakes. To show compassion to others, we first need to practice on ourselves.

Remember, there's no one on this earth who is perfect. Extending grace to others is about showing kindness, even when you feel they don't deserve it.

To extend grace to someone else is simply saying, "Although I don't know everything they've been through, I am willing to be empathetic toward whatever has shaped them into who they are." The quote from the previous page explains it well. As you grow and mature, you will come to understand why extending grace to both yourself and others is so important.

When you make a mistake, don't beat yourself up over it. Try to dig deep and understand why you did what you did. Were you influenced by the wrong crowd? What caused you to act that way? Ask yourself those tough questions and try to uncover the underlying reasons for your actions. Even if you don't have the answers, do yourself a favor and extend yourself grace.

As the late, great Maya Angelou said, "Do the best you can until you know better. Then when you know better, do better."

Today's challenge is to reflect on a situation where you wish you had extended grace to yourself.

Then, think about a time when you could have extended grace to someone else.

Once you've written it down, **apologize to yourself and LET IT GO!**

We may not be able to forget our past, but we can always forgive ourselves for it.

"How you gone win when you aint right within"

Lauren Hill

Day 11

- I am beautiful
- I am loved
- I can do anything I put my mind too
- I am special
- I can overcome any obstacle
- I am destined
- I will not believe negative words
- I am worthy

Today's lesson: Friend or Foe

If you're constantly surrounded by five people who are disrespectful, gossiping, lazy, and disobedient, chances are, you'll become the sixth one. But if you surround yourself with friends who are respectful, focused on growth, and uplifting, then you will grow as well.
We must choose our friendships wisely because they reflect who we are. True friendships should be companions that boost your happiness and reduce stress. Life can be tough and having friends who make you smile and support you through difficult times is beautiful.

The most important aspect of any friendship is **evaluation**.

Ask yourself:
- **Am I surrounded by people who build me up or tear me down?**
- **Do I consider myself to be a true friend?**

If you find yourself gossiping about a friend, ask yourself why. Isn't that your friend? If you hear that your friend has been gossiping about you, don't be so quick to cut ties. Instead, try to understand where they're coming from.

One way to tell if a friend is true is by the comfort level you feel when you are expressing to them what they said or did that hurt you. Hopefully, their response is genuine but if they become rude or upset, then maybe this person's season in your life has expired.

If they apologize, it could mean they care and are willing to change their behavior. But also make sure you aren't contributing to unhealthy habits in the friendship. If you are, this may help you become a better friend going forward.

Although we love sharing secrets with friends, it's important to be careful. Keeping a secret can be difficult for some people, so be cautious about who you trust. With social media being so prevalent, it's often best to keep your business to yourself.

This doesn't mean you're being a "fake" friend—it simply means you're protecting yourself.

As you grow, some people you once called friends may drift apart. They may go to different schools or their role in your life may have been seasonal. But sometimes, when one person gets upset, your secrets can be exposed. None of us are perfect. You may have a best friend who will always be there for you, but you'll also encounter people who are there for a specific purpose.

Appreciate the genuine people who have proven to be real friends and understand that not all relationships are meant to last forever.

CHALLENGE TIME

Friend Evaluation

Start by writing down all your close friends and what they mean to you. Then, list the not-so-good qualities or behaviors they may have.

Next, reflect on why you think you're a good friend and write down times when you haven't been the best friend you could be.

Once you've completed this, take some time to **evaluate, compare, and adjust**.

This is an important part of **Self-Care!**

Day 12

- I am beautiful
- I am loved
- I can do anything I put my mind too
- I am special
- I can overcome any obstacle
- I am destined
- I will not believe negative words
- I am worthy

Today's lesson: Our body is our Temple.

Although we discussed gifts on Day 5, I wanted to touch on another important one.
The first gift any of us was born with is the gift of life. Life is a journey, and when you understand that you have the power to change your circumstances, the obstacles along the way become easier to handle. Realizing that not everyone has access to the knowledge on how to improve, but you do, is something to be grateful for.
Since our body is our temple, we must protect our mind, body, and spirit at all costs. This is your life, and people will break you down mentally, physically, and emotionally, only to walk away feeling uplifted. When you practice positivity and self-control, it will make you a better person.
This doesn't mean you won't snap from time to time, but you will learn to deal with anything when you understand that your mind, body, and soul are sacred. If you wouldn't harm your temple, don't allow anyone else to. As women, we have a sacred gift, the ability to create life. Your virginity is a choice that must be treated with care. If you allow another person to penetrate your temple, ask yourself: *Is this someone I want to carry this memory with?*
Does this guy truly love me? And if I believe that he does, why? Is this the type of guy I want to help raise a child with? Is there mental illness in his family, and will my child be affected by the trauma in his family history? Do his parents believe in healthy relationships, and will they support me if I decide to go to college? Will he get me pregnant and then decide to leave? What are his morals and values?

There are so many things to consider.

Being handsome, cool, or a football star isn't enough of a reason to allow someone to break your temple. *Does he have goals? Do you share the same belief system?* You may be a Christian, and he may be an atheist, or vice versa. *Does his family have a history of cancer or other diseases?* There's so much more to a relationship than simply calling it "love."

Although I also believe that nothing happens by mistake and that we are all here for a reason, why not give yourself the chance to create your own destiny?

Before you give your body away, ask yourself: *Is this someone you can look at ten years from now and accept the journey you both have created?*

The single most important choice you can make is evaluating who you call yourself falling in love with at an early age. Because honestly, you don't even know yourself at this time. Commit to getting to know who you are first and then decide how you want your story to begin.

Day 13

- I am beautiful
- I am loved
- I can do anything I put my mind too
- I am special
- I can overcome any obstacle
- I am destined
- I will not believe negative words
- I am worthy

Story Time

Hello to you all and this is my story

I'm 35 years old, happily married, and have four beautiful kids. When you asked about my story, I jumped at the chance to share because I want to help other women. There were times when I didn't know how I was going to pull through. I've had and still have a great husband, kids, and parents, but nothing could have prepared me for some of the darkest moments in my life. Over time, I've come to realize that those moments have shaped me into who I am today.

Born and raised in Council Bluffs, Iowa, with my siblings, I had what I would consider a great childhood. My mom and dad divorced when I was 4, but they moved on, and I ended up with two moms and two dads. However, my stepmom was difficult to deal with. She was angry and bitter, especially because I was always my daddy's little princess.

Looking back, I can say my parents did a good job with me. I had my ups and downs as a teenager, but I think I turned out well. My stepdad was in the military, and he was a great example for my mom. We all learned how to respect ourselves. He was Native American and Mexican, so we got to experience and learn about different cultures. We learned how to treat others with respect, no matter where they came from. I've taught my kids the same—*we don't see color.*

I have the best husband in the world. He provides for us, ensures we have everything we need, and makes sure that our love is always valued. We've had our share of challenges and have been through a lot together, but we've always known that we love each other, no matter what.

Last year, our 4-year-old daughter was diagnosed with leukemia, but I can say it was a blessing in disguise. We initially went to the hospital because she was having trouble urinating and couldn't have a bowel movement. They found a few other things, but we never thought it would be cancer. That diagnosis caught us completely off guard.

I went to a retreat for help because I was angry with God. Why was this happening to us? I come from a good Christian family with great values. We weren't perfect, but we were a good Christian family, and it didn't seem fair. We battled cancer for three and a half years. I say "we" because we all went through it, but my daughter was the real champion. She took the news better than we did, and she still does.

Through this journey, I had to change my life for the better. What I realized about myself is that I don't want my life to be so structured anymore, I just want peace. I'm truly blessed, and I make sure I put my family first. I attend therapy regularly, and the advice I want to offer you is this: take life slowly.

Think carefully about everything you do before you invest your whole heart in it.

Day 14

- I am beautiful
- I am loved
- I can do anything I put my mind too
- I am special
- I can overcome any obstacle
- I am destined
- I will not believe negative words
- I am worthy

JOURNAL DAY

Spend the day journaling and focusing on you!

MY THOUGHTS

MY THOUGHTS

Day 15

- I am beautiful
- I am loved
- I can do anything I put my mind too
- I am special
- I can overcome any obstacle
- I am destined
- I will not believe negative words
- I am worthy

Today's lesson: Be useful but not used

With age, more than likely comes wisdom. You'll start to question your own character flaws. In my early twenties, I realized that I am an empath. An empath is someone who is highly sensitive and has the ability to sense what others are feeling.

Psychologists describe empaths as individuals who often absorb the pain of others at their own expense. We give away all our energy to make others happy, and in the process, we can feel drained and used. But before we dive into the challenges, let's first talk about the positives.

As an empath, you can walk into any room and instantly connect with strangers, as if you've known them your whole life. You can sense the negative energy in a space and work to shift it, transforming the atmosphere into a more positive one. You listen to understand and offer insightful, uplifting feedback that helps others feel seen and heard.

But there are also some downsides. We often focus more on others than on ourselves, which leads to mental and physical exhaustion, especially when we interact with a lot of people in a short period of time. People tend to recognize who we are and often seek us out for happiness or support. As a result, we may find ourselves being leaned on emotionally, sometimes to the point of feeling drained.

As an empath, it's important to know when to step back. You can't always give advice, and sometimes it's best to let the person figure things out on their own. Most likely, they'll find another listening ear or another empath to lean on.

What can truly irritate your soul is when you give someone advice, only for them to hear the same thing from someone else and then tell you what the other person said. You'll think to yourself, *wait a minute, that's exactly what I told you!*

That should be a clear sign that all your listening and talking was for nothing. Some people don't want advice, they just like to hear themselves talk.

Day 16

- I am beautiful
- I am loved
- I can do anything I put my mind too
- I am special
- I can overcome any obstacle
- I am destined
- I will not believe negative words
- I am worthy

Today's lesson: Hormones

If you haven't already experienced your menstruation (period), you will be experiencing it soon. The primary purpose of your period is to prepare your body for pregnancy and to flush out bacteria from your vaginal canal. If pregnancy does not occur, the uterus sheds its lining.

Sometimes, we may feel depressed, tearful, or moody, not realizing that our bodies are changing. It's important to remind yourself that your hormones are fluctuating. Estrogen and testosterone levels are being tossed around like they're in a trampoline park, which can make you feel upset, angry, or confused. Even as an adult, I still find myself checking my calendar to see if my period is on its way. Your body is going through these changes, and they will continue for a long time. As you get older, you might find yourself crying unexpectedly—even if you're just watching the rain. This is a very emotional, yet sacred time for your body. Your womb is open, so it's best to take only quick showers during this time. The dirty water that filters into our bathtubs isn't ideal, and you want to keep your body as free from unnecessary bacteria as possible.

There's no way to sugarcoat this: just because your body is ready to produce a baby doesn't mean you are mentally ready. Having a baby is one of the most precious moments in a woman's life. You have your whole life ahead of you, and the best decision you can make is to wait until you are mentally and financially prepared to take on the responsibility of raising a child. Having a supportive partner is crucial in this journey. We also need to be mindful of who we choose to have a child with. Were they abused? What are their triggers and traumas? You must ask yourself these questions because the goal is to raise our children with as few traumatic experiences as possible.

Day 17

- I am beautiful
- I am loved
- I can do anything I put my mind too
- I am special
- I can overcome any obstacle
- I am destined
- I will not believe negative words
- I am worthy

Today's lesson: LGBTQ+

Regardless of the gender you identify with, you should always be treated with kindness and respect, just like anyone else. We were all uniquely created and designed, and no one should be mistreated simply because their identity differs from our own. Ultimately, it's none of our business how others identify.
If you're struggling to be accepted by your family or friends, my advice is to limit what you share with them.

No one has the right to bring sadness into your life because of their own biases or misunderstandings. You have so much more to offer, and it's up to you to prove that to yourself. Keep striving to be the best version of you. While society may change over time, not everyone will keep up with that change. What truly matters is your heart. Are you a good person? What are your goals and dreams?
At the end of the day, the people who truly matter will always be there for you—and that's all that really counts.

Always remember that your worth isn't determined by others' opinions. You are valuable just the way you are, and you deserve love, happiness, and respect.

Day 18

- I am beautiful
- I am loved
- I can do anything I put my mind too
- I am special
- I can overcome any obstacle
- I am destined
- I will not believe negative words
- I am worthy

Today's lesson: Grief

Let's begin by defining what grief means.

Grief is the experience of coping with a loss. It's any event that disrupts or challenges our sense of normalcy. Many of us grow up thinking that grief is only linked to death, but there's so much more to it. I want to talk about this because you may not have experienced death yet, but you may have already faced some form of grief.

For example, you might have had a close friend, and for some reason, you stopped talking. Losing that person, depending on how close you were, can bring about grief. You might have been removed from your home, no matter what the reason is, that too can lead to grief. Becoming ill causes grief. Seeing someone you care about struggling with addiction causes grief as well as the person who has checked into a treatment center. Although they made a positive decision, it's still life changing and that could create grief.
Never allow someone to label your grief based on how much pain you show, what they think they know about you, or how severe they perceive your loss to be.

Your grief is yours, and no one has the right to tell you how to feel or when to move on.
Now, death... is incredibly tough.
I've lost several loved ones over the years, and honestly, it hasn't gotten any easier. What I've learned, though, is how to cope with it. The pain cuts deep, and there's nothing we can do to change that.

Most people find ways to cope. Some turn to spirituality, some take the pain out on themselves or others, and some strive to make their deceased loved ones proud. The most important thing I want you to take away from this lesson is the concept of the Five Stages of Grief:
1. **Denial**: It's hard to accept that this has happened.
2. **Anger**: You may become angry at everyone, even a higher power.
3. **Bargaining**: Wishing you could turn back time, trying to negotiate with a higher power.
4. **Depression**: You may feel isolated, detaching from those who love you. This stage can be one of the hardest to overcome.
5. **Acceptance**: While the pain will always be there, you will begin to accept the reality of the loss.

As you can see, there isn't much advice I can give on this topic. I just wanted to make you aware of the stages and encourage you to understand the process of grief, either for yourself or for others who might be experiencing it.

Tips for Coping with the Loss of a Loved One

Dealing with the loss of someone close can feel overwhelming, but there are healthy ways to cope with your emotions. Here are some tips and ideas on how to use coping skills during this difficult time. Remember, there are trained professionals who specialize in helping people navigate grief, and they can offer valuable support as you process your emotions.

Embrace Grief
Allow yourself to feel the pain of your loss. Grief is a natural response, and it's okay to experience a wide range of emotions. Don't suppress what you're feeling; let the grief unfold naturally, in its own time.

Counseling
Sometimes, the most effective way to cope is by talking with a professional. Grief counselors or therapists can help you navigate through the emotional complexities of loss and offer tools to process your feelings.

Journal Your Emotions
Writing down your thoughts can help you understand and release some of the emotions you're dealing with. Journaling provides a safe space for self-expression, and it can help you track your healing process over time.

Embrace Memories
Celebrate the life of your loved one by revisiting positive memories. Whether it's through photos, keepsakes, or just remembering the good times, embracing memories can be a comforting way to honor them.

Express Your Emotions
Don't hold in your feelings. Cry when you need to, talk to others, or engage in activities that allow you to release emotion. Expression, whether through art, music, or physical movement, can be incredibly healing.

Seek Support
Lean on friends, family, or support groups. Connecting with others who understand your pain can help you feel less isolated. There's power in shared experiences.

Participating in Social Activities
While it may feel difficult, gently encourage yourself to engage in social activities. Staying connected with others helps prevent isolation and can offer moments of relief from grief.

Being Kind to Yourself
Grief can be exhausting. Be patient with yourself as you move through the different stages of loss. Take time to rest, nourish your body, and allow yourself the grace to heal at your own pace.

Celebrate Your Loved One's Life
Find ways to celebrate the life your loved one lived. Whether it's through a memorial, creating something in their honor, or simply sharing stories, celebrating their life can bring healing and joy amidst the sorrow.

"Life isn't about waiting for the storm to pass...It's about learning to dance in the rain."

Vivian Greene

Day 19

- I am beautiful
- I am loved
- I can do anything I put my mind too
- I am special
- I can overcome any obstacle
- I am destined
- I will not believe negative words
- I am worthy

Today's lesson: Mental Health

I'm not a psychologist or therapist, so I don't have all the answers. But I want to briefly talk about this topic, because mental health is something we all need to understand.

There are several variations of how mental health is defined, but one is: *a person's condition regarding their psychological and emotional well-being.* Growing up, mental illness was often shunned. When someone was considered "different," most people were afraid to talk about it. When we were struggling with our own mental health as teens, we were often told to "suck it up" or "just get over it." Nobody really wanted to link our behavior to mental health issues. If someone acted out or was "problematic," people would just say, *"Oh, he/she's just crazy."*

We never really stopped to consider what might be going on beneath the surface, because trauma or a chemical imbalance could be at the root of someone's behavior.

Everyone reacts to trauma differently. Trauma can take many forms: molestation, sexual assault, the loss of a parent, divorced parents, homelessness, bullying, low self-esteem, teasing, the list goes on.

There's no shortage of reasons someone might experience pain or struggle.

If you're someone who feels sad every day, it's important to recognize that your mental health might not be in the best shape. Nobody is happy every single day, but if you reach a point where you feel like life isn't worth living, it's time to talk to someone. There is absolutely no shame in seeking help. Life is meant to be lived fully, not just to exist. You are important, and your mental health matters. If there are people around you who bring you down or make you feel less than, it's okay to distance yourself from them.

Every school has a counselor or therapist, and they are there for a reason. Many students are ashamed to use these resources, but they are tools meant to help you. Social workers and counselors can offer support groups and access to resources that can help you cope with your mental health. The same goes for youth detention centers; they also have the tools you can use. Please don't hesitate to reach out for help. Don't give up on yourself.

When you go for years without addressing mental health issues from your childhood, they tend to resurface in adulthood. I know this from experience. In my late twenties, I started trying to heal from childhood trauma. But healing doesn't happen overnight. Sometimes, a song or even a picture will bring back memories I'd rather forget.

You could face rejection, like being denied a job, and suddenly your mind starts to wander back to how you felt when you were rejected as a child. It's also easy for your mental health to slip when you're not paying attention.

Another aspect of mental health is *chemical imbalance*.

A chemical imbalance happens when your brain doesn't have the right levels of neurotransmitters, which help nerve cells communicate. It can happen when there are too many or too few of these chemicals, such as serotonin or norepinephrine. The causes of chemical imbalances aren't always clear, but social and environmental factors can contribute.

Having a chemical imbalance doesn't necessarily mean you will develop a mental health condition, but it can be a factor.

When I started my self-healing journey in my late twenties, I dug deep into my past to better understand who I was and where I came from. I wanted to understand why I made certain decisions. I wondered why I gave my body away at a young age, why I chose to go to certain places, why I felt unworthy growing up. I began meditating, exercising, and praying every day. It was hard work, but it changed me. I lost weight, and I began to feel beautiful, both inside and out.

But here's something I didn't factor into my healing process: just because I was on a journey of self-improvement didn't mean everyone around me was on the same mission. Eventually, I found myself surrounded by the same people, in the same situations, where others would observe my joy and unconsciously try to pull me back down.

Just because you feel like you're overcoming obstacles doesn't mean others will celebrate your growth. Sometimes people want you to stay the same because it's comfortable for them. If you've always been the "rowdy" type, they liked you that way. If you've always been angry, it gave them a reason to distance themselves. But when you change, you break out of the box. You change the mold of what others thought you would become.

This is your life. Your growth isn't seasonal, and it's not for anyone else to control or destroy. The work you put in to improve yourself should be honored, and you shouldn't allow anyone to pull you back into old patterns that no longer serve you.

Day 20

- I am beautiful
- I am loved
- I can do anything I put my mind too
- I am special
- I can overcome any obstacle
- I am destined
- I will not believe negative words
- I am worthy

Story Time

Hello everyone,
Although there are so many layers to my story, I wanted to share a brief version of some of the growing pains I experienced growing up biracial. My mother came from a poor family with 12 siblings, and I was the first biracial child born on the white side of the family, which made me feel like an outsider. I wasn't accepted. I didn't have a relationship with my grandmother because of my skin complexion, and I would often see her do kind things for my cousins but totally neglect me. She would attend their birthday parties but never came to mine. As a child, dealing with that was deeply hurtful and made me feel unwanted. I was too young to understand why I was treated differently.
My mother was white, so, of course, no one knew how to care for my hair, and I just didn't fit in with her side of the family. I wasn't close to my dad's side either, and I spent many years feeling confused, ugly, and afraid.
Once I became a teenager, I started hanging around the wrong crowd because I just wanted to fit in. But I kept my dreams of becoming an actress and a fashion designer in the back of my mind. I used to draw clothing and make little outfits out of different pieces, and I was very creative. However, those dreams took a backseat when I had my first baby.
Having my baby changed my life for the better, but it was tough because I had to transition from being a young girl to a woman very quickly. I wanted to be the best mother I could be and was determined never to let my children feel the way I did growing up. I began to thrive when my baby was born and started to leave childish behavior behind.
Today, at 47, I'm still trying to find my purpose, and I'm just now realizing how much the world has to offer. Although I have social anxiety, I love to travel. Traveling

is something I wish I'd started earlier, but better late than never. I enjoy exploring the world and experiencing new cultures. It's eye-opening and refreshing because it changes your perspective.

Although my mistakes have shaped me for the better, some of the negative ways I used to think about myself still linger from time to time. That's something I work on every day. I'm very protective and private, and I don't allow too many people into my circle. But I do have a close relationship with my mother, my children, and I'm blessed to have great friends. Good friends are hard to come by.

Right now, my children and grandchildren are my focus. Watching my children succeed and accomplish their goals and dreams is what makes me happiest right now.

If I could give you any advice, it would be to stay away from the fellas! (Just kidding.)

But seriously, if I could tell my younger self something, it would be to focus more on myself and stop trying so hard to fit in. Utilize those counselors, adults, and teachers by asking questions about what's out there for you.

Don't waste your time on things that don't matter or on how people feel about you. Focus on your future, and everything else will fall into place.

Day 21

- I am beautiful
- I am loved
- I can do anything I put my mind too
- I am special
- I can overcome any obstacle
- I am destined
- I will not believe negative words
- I am worthy

JOURNAL DAY

Spend the day journaling and focusing on you!

MY THOUGHTS

MY THOUGHTS

Day 22

- I am beautiful
- I am loved
- I can do anything I put my mind too
- I am special
- I can overcome any obstacle
- I am destined
- I will not believe negative words
- I am worthy

Today's lesson: Depression

Sometimes, feeling sad can make us believe that we're depressed. It's important to understand the difference between the two.

Sadness:

- **Temporary Emotion:** Sadness is a natural emotional response to an event or situation, such as loss, disappointment, or a difficult experience. It's a normal part of life and usually fades once the situation improves.

- **Situational:** Sadness typically has a clear cause (e.g., a breakup, failing a class, missing someone).

- **Can Be Managed:** With time and support, you're able to cope and recover.

- **Duration:** Sadness generally lasts a short time, often a few hours to a few days.

Depression:

- **Persistent and Pervasive:** Depression is a much deeper, long-lasting condition that doesn't go away after a few days. It can last for weeks, months, or even years if untreated.

- **Not Always Situational:** Depression doesn't always have a specific cause and can occur even when life seems to be going well.

- **Intense and Overwhelming:** The feelings of sadness are more persistent and can affect almost every aspect of your life, including your energy, thoughts, sleep patterns, and physical health.

- **Symptoms Beyond Sadness:** Depression often includes other symptoms, such as:
    - Loss of interest in things once enjoyed (including hobbies, socializing, creativity)
    - Feelings of worthlessness or guilt
    - Extreme fatigue or lack of energy
    - Difficulty concentrating or making decisions
    - Changes in sleep or appetite (eating too much or too little, sleeping too much or too little)
    - Thoughts of death or suicide (a serious sign of depression that requires immediate attention)
- **Impaired Functioning:** Depression can seriously affect your ability to perform daily tasks or interact with others.
- **Require Treatment:** Unlike sadness, depression often requires professional treatment, such as therapy, counseling, or medication.

In a Nutshell:

- **Sadness** is a normal, temporary feeling that usually passes with time or when the situation improves.
- **Depression**, on the other hand, is a clinical condition that lasts for a long time and affects your overall well-being, often requiring professional help.

It's easy to think that your situation is worse than someone else's. Some people are used as vessels for our blessings and growth, and we often find ourselves asking, "How did they overcome that?" I've seen people compete for the "title" of who has the hardest struggle. The truth is you have no idea what someone else has been through. Some people just make it look easy.

That's why it's important to remind ourselves that we are all battling something, even if it's not visible to the outside world.

One of the main reasons I started exercising is because it boosts endorphins, those happy hormones in the brain.

When endorphins are high, it triggers positive thinking and a general sense of happiness. But when they're low, depression can creep in, bringing feelings of failure, low energy, over or under-eating, and a sense of hopelessness.

We are ALL at risk of depression!

While there are tons of professionals out there to assist us on our life journey, it's also crucial to take control and hold ourselves accountable for maintaining our mental health. You can be the most beautiful person on the outside, but if your mental health isn't in a good place, you might feel like the ugliest duckling on the planet.

Never compare your life to someone else's. Drink plenty of water, mind your business, and take care of your mind. If that means seeking professional help, please do and never be ashamed. You only have one life, and it's important that you strive to be the best version of yourself, right now, and as soon as possible. It will take time, but trust me, you got this, girl.

Day 23

- I am beautiful
- I am loved
- I can do anything I put my mind too
- I am special
- I can overcome any obstacle
- I am destined
- I will not believe negative words
- I am worthy

FUN ACTIVITY TIME:

Let's Get to Work on Your Gifts and Goals!

This activity is all about **researching** and **planning** to turn your gifts and passions into real career opportunities.

So, let's dive right in! Here's your list of tasks and steps to take to bring you closer to your goals:

1. Research Your Career Interests
Start by **looking online** or going to the **library** to gather information on the profession you're interested in. You want to learn everything you can, including:

- **Career statistics**: What is the job outlook? How many people are currently employed in this field? Are jobs growing or declining?

- **Salary information**: How much can you expect to earn in this profession? What are the starting salaries, and what could you earn as you gain experience?

- **Required qualifications**: What education or certifications are needed? Do you need a degree, training, or special skills?

- **Daily life of the job**: What does a typical day look like? What kind of tasks or responsibilities will you have?

2. Make Your Dream Known

After you've done some research, show an adult that you're serious about your goal. This could be a mentor, teacher, or someone you trust. Explain what you've found and your passion for pursuing this career

Sidenote: Having someone else involved in your process can hold you accountable, plus they might offer valuable advice or connections!

3. Study the Greats!

Have you studied the people who have succeeded in your field? Look up interviews, books, podcasts, or documentaries about the greats who've walked the path before you.

Understand their:
- Struggles and how they overcame them
- Steps they took to get where they are
- Strategies for success
- The habits and mindset that helped them.

Studying successful people will help you understand the journey ahead and give you inspiration to push forward.

4. Plan B: What's Your Backup?

What's your Plan B? Life doesn't always go according to plan, and things may not work out with your first choice. It's important to have a **second career option** in case things don't pan out or you lose interest over time.
For example:
- If your first choice is to become a lawyer but later you feel that it's not your passion anymore, you can pick out your plan B. Maybe even a Plan C. The more plans the merrier.

5. Set a Timeline
How long will it take to accomplish your goal? Setting a **realistic timeline** helps you stay focused. Break down your long-term goal into **short-term milestones**.
For example:
- If you want to be a lawyer, what's the time commitment for law school? How long will it take you to pass the bar exam?

6. Act Now
What are some **steps you can take today** to bring you closer to your goal? Start with small actions to get the ball rolling:
- For example, if you want to be a **hair stylist**, maybe your first step is researching local beauty schools. What is the application process?
- If you want to be a **dancer**, look up nearby dance classes and sign up for one to shadow an instructor.
- For a **professional athlete**, begin improving your skills, attend tryouts, or join a local team.

Every little action will help you inch closer to your dream!

7. Is It a Gift, Career, or Both?
Sometimes your passion might be a **gift** that isn't your main career (yet). You might have to work in a different field while perfecting your gift until it becomes your primary focus.
For example:
- **My profession is nursing**, but my passion is writing. In order to take care of myself financially, I work as a nurse. While I enjoy helping others in healthcare, my goal is to become a bestselling author, and I'm working toward that every day.

Example Career Paths to Explore

Here are some examples of professions you can research, based on your interests:

- **Attorney**: Ask yourself: What fascinates you about law? How long will it take to complete your education? What's the average salary? What kind of classes or internships will you need?
- **Hair Stylist**: Dream of becoming the best stylist in your city? Research what it takes to become a top-tier stylist.
- **News Anchor/Journalist**: Do you have a passion for speaking or writing? Explore how to break into the world of journalism or broadcasting. You might need to work in local media first to build your portfolio.
- **Professional Athlete**: If you're aiming for the big leagues, research how to get recruited or gain experience. You may have to start by joining a sports team, going to tryouts, or building your social media presence.
- **Singer/Dancer**: Pursue performing arts! Look for audition opportunities, singing/dancing classes, or open-mic events. Practice makes perfect!
- **Life Coach or Public Speaker**: Are you well-spoken and inspiring? You could become a life coach or motivational speaker. Consider taking coaching courses and learning from other speakers in your field.
- **Politician (Senator, Mayor, etc.)**: If you want to make a difference in your community, consider a career in public service. Start by volunteering, attending local government meetings, and learning about what it takes to run for office.
- **Community Leader**: If you care about bringing change to your neighborhood, you might want to start a nonprofit, work with local leaders, or create social movements.

Final Thought:

Take Your First Step Today!
The journey to success isn't a straight line, and you might hit a few bumps along the way.

Researching, and setting realistic goals will move you closer to where you want to be.

You're not just dreaming, you're building a future. So go ahead and get started on your path today! You've got this!

The Next Step: Shadowing a Professional!

Now that you've done the research, it's time to take the next step: Shadowing

Shadowing someone in the profession you want to pursue is a great way to gain real-world insight into your future career and make valuable connections with people who can help you along the way.

Here's a guide that will help you make the most of this experience:

1. Ask an Adult to Help with the Connection
Reach out to the adult you've spoken to about your career interests and ask them to contact someone in the field you want to shadow. Most professionals love giving back to young adults and helping them succeed. It not only benefits you, but it also helps professionals feel good knowing they are making a positive impact.

Tip: Be specific when asking. For example, if you want to shadow a nurse, let the adult know that you're interested in a specific hospital or specialty within nursing.

2. Prepare for the Shadowing Experience

Before you meet with the professional, you're shadowing, make sure you're fully prepared:

Write Down Questions
Think about what you want to know about their career. Here are some example questions you could ask:

- What does your typical day look like?
- How did you get started in this career?
- What is the most rewarding part of your job?
- What are the biggest challenges you face?
- What skills or education did you need to succeed in this field?
- What advice do you have for someone just starting out?
- Is there anything about this job that you wish you had known earlier?

Be Ready to Listen
You're there to **learn**, so make sure you're actively listening to everything the professional shares. Take notes if you need to. This will help you retain the information and reflect on it later.

3. Be Prompt, Courteous, and Assertive
Your **first impression** is key, so make sure you're on time and respectful. Here's how to make a great impression:

- **Be on time**: Arrive early or exactly on time. It shows that you're serious and value the professional's time.
- **Be courteous**: Say "thank you" when you meet and after the shadowing experience is over. Simple manners go a long way.
- **Be assertive**: Don't be afraid to ask questions and engage with the professional. Show that you're interested and eager to learn. Ask for feedback on how you can improve or prepare better for your career.

4. Limit Distractions
When you're shadowing, you want to be fully present. That means leaving your cell phone out of sight unless you're asked to look something up. This shows respect for the professional's time and ensures you're focused on learning.

5. Reflect After the Experience
After you finish shadowing, take time to reflect on the experience:

- **What did you learn** that you didn't know before?
- **What surprised you** about the job or the career path?
- **Do you still feel excited** about pursuing this profession?
- **What steps** can you take next to continue progressing toward your goal?

6. Follow Up with Gratitude
Once you've finished the shadowing experience, make sure to thank the professional for taking the time to help you. You can do this with a short, polite thank-you email or handwritten note. Gratitude goes a long way, and it can even help you keep a good connection for future opportunities!

Final Thoughts
Shadowing a professional will give you the opportunity to see your future career up close and personal.

It will provide valuable insight that research alone can't offer, and it will help you decide if this is the right path for you.

Remember, don't be afraid to ask questions and take full advantage of this opportunity to learn and grow. This experience will fuel your desire to succeed and make your dreams feel even more achievable.

Day 24

- I am beautiful
- I am loved
- I can do anything I put my mind too
- I am special
- I can overcome any obstacle
- I am destined
- I will not believe negative words
- I am worthy

Today's lesson: DRUGS

When it comes to understanding substance abuse and addiction, I believe that while education through a degree is important, nothing beats real life experience.

If you've witnessed family members smoking cigarettes, you may be more likely to start smoking. If you've seen friends and family members struggle with substances like marijuana, crack, heroin, or alcohol, and you've managed to stay away from those things despite the pressure, then you've already overcome major odds.

Drugs and alcohol are often used to numb the pain whether it's emotional, physical, or mental. It's easy to judge others for their addictions, especially our elders, but we rarely stop to ask, "What led them to start these habits in the first place?"

Growing up, we were told to say no to drugs, and we learned about their effects on our brains, but why do some people still turn to them?

I remember a seasoned crack user once told me, "Baby, it takes just one hit." When he said that, I knew he was speaking from experience. And yet, even knowing that, why do we believe we'll be the exception? Why do we think that we can try something once and never get hooked?

Think about what you stand to lose.
My advice is simple: Think about what drugs and alcohol would jeopardize in your life right now. What could you lose if you gave in to the temptation? It's easy to blame our struggles on external factors and convince ourselves

that using substances will hide the pain. But what does that really do in the long run?

I'm telling you from my own experience that once you start using substances to numb the pain, you'll begin to depend on them just to get through the day. That's why addiction is called "dependence" because, eventually, you'll rely on the substance just to function.

Did you know that tobacco is one of the hardest addictions to break? Many people roll marijuana in tobacco leaves, thinking they're avoiding cigarettes, but they're still getting hooked on nicotine. It's a vicious cycle. Your body enjoys marijuana, but the nicotine addiction follows right behind.

When adults say, "Say no to drugs," it's because they love you and understand how incredibly difficult it is to break free from addiction. If you're reading this and you're struggling with addiction, I want you to know that you can change.

Try meditating and reflect on how much you want to overcome this and take it one step at a time. It's not easy, but it's possible. Everything starts in your mind, and if you've made it this far in this book, it means you have the desire to change. You are worthy of a better life, and I believe in you.

There's nothing wrong with enjoying a casual drink once you reach adulthood. Alcohol can be a social relaxer and stress reliever, but moderation is key.

Remember: balance is everything. Never underestimate the power of addiction, because once it takes hold, it can be incredibly hard to shake. So, always take a step back and think about what really matters before diving into anything that could change the course of your life.

Day 25

- I am beautiful
- I am loved
- I can do anything I put my mind too
- I am special
- I can overcome any obstacle
- I am destined
- I will not believe negative words
- I am worthy

Today's lesson: Social Media

Social media can be both a blessing and a curse for all of us. It's incredibly influential—not only for young people but for adults as well. One of the biggest concerns we have for young women today is the unrealistic beauty standards that are relentlessly promoted online. Every day, we see posts comparing skin tones, and videos circulating about who's the prettiest—light-skinned or dark-skinned. Let me say this loud and clear: You have NOTHING to prove to anyone.

We all love to scroll through our feeds and admire the beautiful people we see online, but here's the truth: No one looks like that every single day. There are filters, and behind some of those smiles, there are tears. Social media isn't always what it seems. Then there are those who share every little detail of their lives on Facebook, Twitter, and Instagram. While some might think it's cathartic, I believe there's a time and place for privacy, especially when you're dealing with sorrow or pain.

Think about it: What can people do with your personal struggles, besides gossip about you or use your pain as entertainment? The more you expose about yourself, the more others have to use against you.

If your goal is to be an influencer or simply have a positive presence online, try your best to stay as positive as possible. And if you ever find yourself having a rough day and wanting to vent, my advice is simply log off. There are people out there who would love nothing more than to see you act out or make a fool of yourself. Social media can be a trap, so it's important to stay grounded.

Keep your business private, network, and connect with others on social media, but don't get fooled by the fakeness of it all. Social media is not the whole picture of anyone's life.

Stay true to who you are and never forget that the person in the mirror is the real beauty, no filter required.

And remember: **Don't sign up to be a clown in the social media circus.**

Day 26

- I am beautiful
- I am loved
- I can do anything I put my mind too
- I am special
- I can overcome any obstacle
- I am destined
- I will not believe negative words
- I am worthy

Today's lesson: Spirituality/Prayer

Let me give you my best definition of what spirituality truly means. It's when you have a mental battle within yourself, and something inside of you is saying, "This decision isn't right." That voice, that feeling, is your spirituality in action.

We were all blessed with the gift of tuning into our mind, body, and soul. When you feel that inner voice telling you, "Don't do it," or hear the echo of advice from your parents or an elder, urging you, "That's not good for you," listen to it.

I'm writing this book for people from all walks of life, so I'm not here to force any specific religion on you. What I am here to encourage is that you choose to trust that inner voice—because that voice is the voice of **God**. We all have the power to listen to the voice of reason, to the voice of power. It's the voice that helps you distinguish right from wrong. When you ignore it, the consequences are often hard to avoid.

You never know who is blessed with spiritual discernment. A homeless person who lives on the street can offer some life-changing advice.

Spiritual discernment, as defined by spiritualgifttest.com, is the ability to "distinguish between spirits." It's the gift of knowing what is of God and what is not.

People may not have made the right choices in their own lives, but don't judge them. They may be telling you this for a reason. Sometimes, people can show you the right path simply because they've made the wrong turn before. If you judge them based on their mistakes, you could miss the very message God is trying to send you.

Whatever God you believe in, just know that He often sends his messengers to guide you.

If you choose not to listen, you cannot blame anyone but yourself. The power to make wise decisions is within you. Tap into it.

Day 27

- I am beautiful
- I am loved
- I can do anything I put my mind too
- I am special
- I can overcome any obstacle
- I am destined
- I will not believe negative words
- I am worthy

Story Time

When I was a young girl, I was insecure about my skin complexion. I could feel jealousy from my peers and family because they were darker-skinned. My mother was often mean to me, and I always thought it was because people would tell me that I looked just like her. Now that I'm grown, I realize that she didn't like herself. Seeing my face reminded her of all the mistakes she had made in her past.

My dream was to become a dancer and a stylist. I didn't think I was pretty when I was younger because I had big eyes, big lips, and people would say I had a big forehead. But now, as I've gotten older, people are paying for the physical attributes I once hated.

My godmother was the one person I honestly felt truly loved me. She would always hug me, love on me, and make me feel so special.

I waited to become sexually active for a long time because my mother and her siblings were teenage mothers, and I didn't want to make the same mistake. I was scared to become a mother because of the generational curses in my family. For example, one curse I wanted to break was learning how to communicate. My mother didn't communicate with me, and I felt so unloved. I wasn't sure if I would repeat the same patterns, and I often promised myself, "I'm going to do better when I get older." Another curse was how some of my cousins became lost in the foster system.

My mother's distrust of me kept her from supporting my dreams or even letting me be a regular teenager. I wanted to go skating and have fun, but her fears kept me sheltered. She was afraid I would make the same mistakes she did, and I used to beg her to trust me.

I was introduced to the foster care system when my cousins' children were taken away. I didn't want to see them go into the system, so I moved into a three-bedroom house so I could take them in, even though I didn't have children of my own yet. After completing all the requirements to become a foster parent, I was told I needed more space and couldn't take them in. Later, however, I did become a foster parent.

I became a mother at 28 years old, unexpectedly, by a man who was older than me, and our relationship was strictly sexual. That wasn't the plan I had for myself, but I'm grateful for my son. His father wasn't active, but he did pay child support. Still, I wouldn't take that experience back for anything in the world.

If I could give you any advice, it would be to get to know yourself, set goals, and figure out what you want to do before having children.

I prayed about my relationship with my mother, hoping that one day we could develop mutual respect. My fear was that we would never be able to rekindle our relationship and one of us would pass away before we had the chance. I now realize that there's always room to change any situation. You have to learn how to open your heart because being cold-hearted will never help you grow.

Today, I'm blessed to say that my mother and I have developed a beautiful friendship, and for that, I am thankful.

Day 28

- I am beautiful
- I am loved
- I can do anything I put my mind too
- I am special
- I can overcome any obstacle
- I am destined
- I will not believe negative words
- I am worthy

JOURNAL DAY

Spend the day journaling and focusing on you!

MY THOUGHTS

MY THOUGHTS

"Empowerment begins with embracing your strengths and acknowledging your weaknesses. By celebrating who you are and recognizing where you can grow, you cultivate the self-esteem, image, and efficacy needed to conquer any challenge. Believe in your power, and watch yourself soar"

Kara Warner

Day 29

- I am beautiful
- I am loved
- I can do anything I put my mind too
- I am special
- I can overcome any obstacle
- I am destined
- I will not believe negative words
- I am worthy

Today's lesson: Foster Care/Group Home Youth Center

Let me give you a little background on how foster care became what it is today.

In 1853, Charles Loring Brace launched the free foster home movement. As a minister and the director of the New York Children's Aid Society, Brace was deeply concerned about the large number of immigrant children sleeping on the streets of New York City.

In response, he devised a plan to offer these children homes by advertising in the South and West, seeking families willing to take them in. These families were motivated either for charitable reasons or the potential benefits these children could offer.

While many of these children were placed in conditions resembling indentured servitude, Brace's bold and innovative actions ultimately laid the foundation for the modern foster care system.
(*NFPA: History of Foster Care in the US, 2024*)

Indentured Servitude refers to a labor contract where a person works for a set period without pay to repay a debt, loan, or as compensation for a service or good.

I'm glad to see that the foster care system has evolved. Although you may not have had a choice of where you were initially placed, you do have a voice in whether you stay there. You are your own advocate. If you feel mistreated, violated, or unheard in your home, please tell your social worker or foster care specialist immediately. Living under those conditions is unacceptable. However, if you're in a home where there is food, water, shelter, and safety, you are in a great space.

As adults, opening our homes to foster children can feel intimidating. We understand how difficult life was for you before coming into our home, and we recognize the trauma involved in the transition.

I've been a foster parent for a few years now, and while it's a joy to have kids live with me, the transition is challenging for me as well.

We must get to know you, and if I could speak for all the good foster parents out there in the world, we hope and pray that we are doing the best we can to make you feel safe and welcomed.

I know it's hard being away from family, no matter the reason. I want you to know that it's okay to feel angry about your situation because it's not your fault. Even if your behavior wasn't the best and you were court-ordered, don't be hard on yourself. Life is a journey, and some things happen for a reason. The older you get, the more you'll realize that everyone carries something they will spend a lifetime healing from. Healing doesn't happen overnight; it takes one day at a time.

If you find yourself in a great home, try your best to give your foster parent some grace. Remember we talked about the meaning of grace on day ten. Transitioning can be tough for everyone, but if you are in a bad situation, advocate for yourself.

The system is designed to protect you. If you're about to transition out of foster care, use the resources available to you.

They can help you find a job and housing. This is your life, and not only do I want you to advocate for safety, but I also want you to advocate for growth. There are scholarships for college and other advantages. Talk to your social worker, foster care agency, and foster parent. Let's start adulthood by making the best choices so you can live abundantly.

Some of us grew up in families where criminal activity seemed normal.

Some of us hung out with friends who thought it was cool to end up in a detention center.
The truth is, traveling down that path, no matter how we got there, is a long, bumpy road.

Over time, it becomes harder to change your behavior. It may start to feel like making the right decisions is a far-off goal.

What usually happens is that, as you get older, you may start to believe there's nothing else out there, so why even try?

If this describes you, or if you know someone in this situation, I want to encourage you that it's never too late. Take those bad decisions as lessons.

Everything we experience in life has a lesson, whether it's good or bad. If you're currently in a detention center or group home, remember that this is only temporary. Changing your behavior starts with your mindset and the way you speak about yourself. Instead of saying, "I can't do this," say, "I'm going to figure this out." Instead of saying, "Nobody cares about me," say, "I'm going to vow to care about myself, even if nobody else shows me they care."

Respect whatever situation you're in right now. If you're in a detention center or group home, wake up and speak to the staff. Smile when you look in the mirror, because this is the person you'll be stuck with for the rest of your life.

Instead of sitting around doing nothing, pick up a book. Choose one that interests you. Reading feeds your mind and allows you to live outside the box for a moment. Don't worry about your friends and family right now, just choose yourself.

When you talk to them, speak positively about yourself and let them know that you've decided to do better and that you're going to start now.

If you're reading this and it's not your situation, show this chapter to someone who you think may need it.

Day 30

- I am beautiful
- I am loved
- I can do anything I put my mind too
- I am special
- I can overcome any obstacle
- I am destined
- I will not believe negative words
- I am worthy

MISSION COMPLETE

LET'S TALK ABOUT IT

Did you enjoy this journal?

Are there any lessons that helped you?

What changes do you plan on making?

Thank you for taking the time to read through this journal. Not only does completing this benefit you, but it also brings me joy, knowing that you've taken the steps to complete this 30-day process.

I hope you continue to keep this as a reminder and make it a habit to write in it every day. Journaling is a powerful tool, just like you. Take control of your destiny, feed your mind with positivity, and set those boundaries. By doing so, you'll be setting yourself up for success.

MY JOURNAL

MY JOURNAL

MY JOURNAL

MY JOURNAL

MY JOURNAL

MY JOURNAL

MY JOURNAL

MY JOURNAL

MY JOURNAL

MY JOURNAL

MY JOURNAL

MY JOURNAL

MY JOURNAL

MY JOURNAL

MY JOURNAL

MY JOURNAL

MY JOURNAL

MY JOURNAL

MY JOURNAL

MY JOURNAL

MY JOURNAL

MY JOURNAL

MY JOURNAL

MY JOURNAL

MY JOURNAL

MY JOURNAL

MY JOURNAL

MY JOURNAL

MY JOURNAL

MY JOURNAL

MY JOURNAL

MY JOURNAL

MY JOURNAL

MY JOURNAL

MY JOURNAL

MY JOURNAL

MY JOURNAL

MY JOURNAL

MY JOURNAL

MY JOURNAL

MY JOURNAL

MY JOURNAL